As A Man Thinketh

AS A

MAN THINKETH

James Allen's

Greatest Inspirational Essays

Edited by William B. Franklin and William R. Webb

Illustrated by Bruce Baker

♔ HALLMARK CROWN EDITIONS

"The Importance of Self-Government,"
"The Three Stages of Self-Discipline,"
and "The Virtue of Self-Discipline"
from Above Life's Turmoil by James Allen.
Reprinted by permission of G. P. Putnam's Sons.
"Thought and Character"
reprinted by permission of the National Council
of the Churches of Christ
from the Revised Standard Version Bible.

CONTENTS

WHO WAS JAMES ALLEN?

by William R. Webb

JAMES ALLEN is a literary mystery man. His inspirational writings have influenced millions for good. Yet today he remains almost unknown.

None of his nineteen books gives a clue to his life other than to mention his place of residence—Ilfracombe, England. His name cannot be found in a major reference work. Not even the Library of Congress or the British Museum has much to say about him.

Who was this man who believed in the power of thought to bring fame, fortune and happiness? Was he able to help others, but not himself? Or did he, as Henry David Thoreau says, "hear a different drummer"?

James Allen never gained fame or fortune. That much is true. His was a quiet, unrewarded genius. He seldom made enough money from his writings to cover expenses.

Allen was born in Leicester, Central England, November 28, 1864. The family business failed within a few years, and in 1879 his father left for America in an effort to recoup his losses. The elder Allen had hoped to settle in the United States, but was robbed and murdered before he could send for his family.

The financial crisis that resulted forced James to leave school at fifteen. He eventually became a private secretary, a position that would be called "administrative assistant" today. He worked in this capacity for several British manufacturers until 1902, when he decided to devote all his time to writing.

Unfortunately, Allen's literary career was short, lasting only nine years, until his death in 1912. During that period he wrote nineteen books, a rich outpouring of ideas that have lived on to inspire later generations.

Soon after finishing his first book, *From Poverty To Power*, Allen moved to Ilfracombe, on England's southwest coast. The little resort town with its seafront Victorian hotels and its rolling hills and winding lanes offered him the quiet atmosphere he needed to pursue his philosophical studies.

As A Man Thinketh was Allen's second book. Despite its subsequent popularity he was dissatisfied with it. Even though it was his most concise and eloquent work, the book that best embodied his thought, he somehow failed to recognize its value. His wife Lily had to persuade him to publish it.

James Allen strove to live the ideal life described by Russia's great novelist and mystic Count Leo Tolstoy—the life of voluntary poverty, manual labor and ascetic self-discipline. Like Tolstoy, Allen sought to improve himself, be happy, and master all of the virtues. His search for "felicity for man on earth" was typically Tolstoyan.

According to his wife, Allen "wrote when he had a message, and it became a message only when he had lived it in his own life, and knew that it was good."

His day in Ilfracombe began with a predawn walk up to the Cairn, a stony spot on the hillside overlooking his home and the sea. He would remain there for an hour in meditation. Then he would return to the house and spend the morning writing. The afternoons were devoted to gardening, a pastime he enjoyed. His evenings were spent in conversation with those who were interested in his work.

A friend described Allen as "a frail-looking little man, Christ-like, with a mass of flowing black hair."

"I think of him especially in the black velvet suit he always wore in the evenings," the friend wrote. "He would talk quietly to a small group of us then—English, French, Austrian and Indian—of meditation, of philosophy, of Tolstoy or Buddha, and of killing nothing, not even a mouse in the garden.

"He overawed us all a little because of his appearance, his gentle conversation, and especially because he went out to commune with God on the hills before dawn."

James Allen's philosophy became possible when liberal Protestantism discarded the stern dogma that man is sinful by nature. It substituted for that dogma an optimistic belief in man's innate goodness and divine rationality.

This reversal of doctrine was, as William James said, the greatest revolution of the 19th Century. It was part of a move toward a reconciliation between science and religion following Darwin's publication of *The Origin of Species*.

Charles Darwin himself hinted at the change in belief in *The Descent of Man*. In that book he wrote, "the highest possible stage in moral culture is when we recognize that we ought to control our thoughts."

Allen's work embodies the influence of Protestant liberalism on the one hand and of Buddhist thought on the other. For example, the Buddha teaches, "All that we are is the result of what we have thought." Allen's Biblical text says, "As a man thinketh in his heart, so is he."

Allen insists upon the power of the individual to form his own character and to create his own happiness. "Thought and

character are one," he says, "and as character can only manifest and discover itself through environment and circumstance, the outer conditions of a person's life will always be found to be harmoniously related to his inner state. This does not mean that a man's circumstances at any given time are an indication of his entire character, but that those circumstances are so intimately connected with some vital thought element within him that, for the time being, they are indispensable to his development."

Allen starts us thinking—even when we would rather be doing something else. He tells us how thought leads to action. He shows us how to turn our dreams into realities.

His is a philosophy that has brought success to millions. It is the philosophy of Norman Vincent Peale's *The Power of Positive Thinking* and of Joshua Liebman's *Peace of Mind*.

We become spiritually rich, Allen writes, when we discover the adventure within; when we are conscious of the oneness of all life; when we know the power of meditation; when we experience kinship with nature.

Allen's message is one of hope even in the midst of confusion. "Yes," he says, "humanity surges with uncontrolled passion, is tumultuous with ungoverned grief, is blown about by anxiety and doubt. Only the wise man, only he whose thoughts are controlled and purified, makes the winds and the storms of the soul obey him."

"Tempest-tossed souls," Allen continues, "wherever you may be, under whatsoever conditions you may live, know this —in the ocean of life the isles of blessedness are smiling and the sunny shore of your ideal awaits your coming. . . ."

And thus Allen teaches two essential truths: today we are where our thoughts have taken us, and we are the architects— for better or worse—of our futures.

AS A MAN THINKETH

THOUGHT AND CHARACTER

Finally, brethren, whatever is true,
whatever is honorable,
whatever is just,
whatever is pure, whatever is lovely,
whatever is gracious, . . .
think about these things.

PHILIPPIANS 4:8 (RSVB)

THE APHORISM "As a man thinketh in his heart, so is he," embraces the whole of a man's being. It is so comprehensive that it reaches out to every condition and circumstance of life. A man is literally what he thinks. His character is the sum of all his thoughts.

As the plant springs from the seed, and could not be without it, so every act of a man springs from the hidden seeds of thought. This truth applies as equally to those acts called "spontaneous" as to those which are deliberate.

Act is the blossom of thought, and joy and suffering are its fruits; thus a man harvests the sweet and bitter fruits of his own husbandry.

Man is a growth by law, and not a creation by artifice, for cause and effect is as absolute and undeviating in the hidden realm of thought as in the world of visible and material things.

A noble character is not a thing of favor or chance, but the natural result of continued effort in right thinking, the effect of long-cherished association with noble thoughts. An ignoble and bestial character, by the same process, is the result of the continued harboring of sensual thoughts.

A man's mind is like a garden, which may be intelligently cultivated or allowed to run wild. But whether cultivated or neglected, it must, and will, bring forth. If no useful seeds are put into it, then an abundance of useless weed seeds will fall into it, and will continue to produce their useless kind.

Just as a gardener cultivates his plot, keeping it free from weeds, and grows the flowers and fruits which he needs, so may a man tend the garden of his mind, weeding out all the wrong, useless, and impure thoughts, and cultivating all the right, useful, and pure thoughts. By this process, a man sooner or later discovers that he is the master gardener of his soul, the director of his life. He also reveals, within himself, the laws of thought, and understands, with ever-increasing accuracy, how thought forces and mind elements operate in shaping his character, circumstances, and destiny.

Thought and character are one, and as character can only manifest and discover itself through environment and circumstance, the outer conditions of a person's life will always be found to be harmoniously related to his inner state. This does not mean that a man's circumstances at any given time are an indication of his entire character, but that those circumstances are so intimately connected with some vital thought element within him that, for the time being, they are indispensable to his development.

Every man is where he is by the law of his being. The thoughts which he has built into his character have brought him there, and in the arrangement of his life there is no element of chance. All is the result of a law which cannot err. This is just as true of those who feel "out of harmony" with their surroundings as of those who are contented with them.

Man is made or unmade by himself. In the armory of thought he forges the weapons by which he destroys himself. He also fashions the tools with which he builds for himself heavenly mansions of joy and strength and peace. By the right choice and true application of thought, man ascends to divine perfection. By the abuse and wrong application of thought, he descends below the level of the beast. Between these two are all the grades of character, and man is their maker and master.

Of all the beautiful truths pertaining to the soul, none is more gladdening or fruitful of divine promise and confidence than this—that man is the master of thought, the molder of character, and the maker and shaper of condition, environment, and destiny.

HAPPINESS IS A STATE OF MIND

Our life is what we make it by our own thoughts and deeds. It is our own state and attitude of mind which determine whether we are happy or unhappy, strong or weak, sinful or holy, foolish or wise. If one is unhappy, that state of mind belongs to himself, and is originated within himself; it is a state which responds to certain outward happenings, but its *cause* lies within, and not in those outward occurrences. If one is weak in will, he has brought himself to, and remains in, that condition by the course of thought and action which he has chosen and is still choosing. If one is sinful, it is because he has committed, and continues to commit, sinful acts. If he is foolish, it is because he himself does foolish things.

A man has no character, no soul, no life apart from his thoughts and deeds. What they are, that he is. As they are modified, so does he change. He is endowed with will, and can modify his character. As the carpenter changes the block of wood into a beautiful piece of furniture, so can the erring and sin-stricken man change himself into a wise and truth-loving being.

MAN AS MIND

Man is; and as he thinks, so he is. A perception and realization of these two facts alone—of man's being and thinking—lead into a vast avenue of knowledge which cannot stop short of the highest wisdom and perfection. One of the reasons why men do not become wise is that they occupy themselves with interminable speculations about a *soul* separate from themselves— that is, from their own mind—and so blind themselves to their actual nature and being. The supposition of a separate soul veils the eyes of man so that he does not see himself, does not know his mentality, is unaware of the nature of his thoughts without which he would have no conscious life.

Man cannot be separated from his mind; his life cannot be separated from his thoughts. Mind, thought, and life are as inseparable as light, radiance, and color, and are no more in need of another factor to elucidate them than are light, radiance, and color. The facts are all-sufficient, and contain within themselves the groundwork of all knowledge concerning them.

Man as mind is subject to change. He is not something "made" and finally completed, but has within him the capacity for progress. By the universal law of evolution he has *become* what he is, and is becoming that which he will be. His being is modified by every thought he thinks. Every experience affects his character. Every effort he makes changes his mentality. Herein is the secret of man's degradation, and also of his power and salvation if he but utilize this law of change in the right choice of thought.

To live is to think and act, and to think and act is to change. While man is ignorant of the nature of thought, he continues to change for better or worse; but, being acquainted with the nature of thought, he intelligently accelerates and directs the process of change, and only for the better.

What the sum total of a man's thoughts are, that he is. From this sameness of thought with man there is not the slightest fractional deviation. There is a change of result with the addition and subtraction of thought, but the mathematical law is an invariable quantity.

DIGNITY AND SELF-DISCIPLINE

He who reigns within himself,
and rules passions,
desires, and fears,
is more than a king.

JOHN MILTON

A MAN does not *live* until he begins to discipline himself; he merely *exists*. Like an animal he gratifies his desires and pursues his inclinations just where they may lead him. He is happy as a beast is happy, because he is not conscious of what he is depriving himself; he suffers as the beast suffers, because he does not know the way out of suffering. He does not intelligently reflect upon life, and lives in a series of sensations, longings, and confused memories which are unrelated to any central idea or principle. A man whose inner life is so ungoverned and chaotic must necessarily manifest this confusion in the visible conditions of his outer life in the world; and though for a time, running with the stream of his desires, he may draw to himself a more or less large share of the outer necessities and comforts of life, he never achieves any real success nor accomplishes any real good, and sooner or later worldly failure and disaster are inevitable, as the direct result of the inward failure to properly adjust and regulate those mental forces which make the outer life.

Before a man can accomplish anything of an enduring nature in the world he must first of all acquire some measure of success in the management of his own mind. This is as mathematical a truism as that two and two are four, for "out of the heart are the issues of life." If a man cannot govern the forces within himself, he cannot long hold a firm hand upon the outer activities which form his visible life. On the other hand, as a man succeeds in governing himself he rises to higher and higher levels of power and usefulness and success in the world.

The only difference between the life of the beast and that of the undisciplined man is that the man has a wider variety of desires, and experiences a greater intensity of suffering. It may be said of such a man that he is dead, being truly dead to self-control, chastity, fortitude, and all the nobler qualities which constitute *life*.

THE THREE STAGES OF SELF-DISCIPLINE

With the practice of self-discipline a man begins to live, for he then commences to rise above the inward confusion and to adjust his conduct to a steadfast center within himself. He ceases to follow where inclination leads him, reins in the steed of his desires, and lives in accordance with the dictates of reason and wisdom. Hitherto his life has been without purpose or meaning, but now he begins to consciously mold his own destiny; he is "clothed and in his right mind."

In the process of self-discipline there are three stages, namely:

1. Control
2. Purification
3. Relinquishment

A man begins to discipline himself by controlling those passions which have hitherto controlled him; he resists temptation, and guards himself against all those tendencies to selfish gratifications which are so easy and natural, and which have formerly dominated him. He brings his appetite into subjection, and begins to eat as a reasonable and responsible being, practicing moderation and thoughtfulness in the selection of his food, with the object of making his body a pure instrument through which he may live and act as becomes a man, and no longer degrading that body by pandering to gustatory pleasure. He puts a check upon his tongue, his temper, and, in fact, his every animal desire and tendency, and this he does by referring all his acts to a fixed center within himself. It is a process of living from within outward, instead of, as formerly, from without inward. He conceives of an ideal, and, enshrining that ideal in the sacred recesses of his heart, he regulates his conduct in accordance with its exactions and demands.

There is a philosophical hypothesis that at the heart of every atom and every aggregation of atoms in the universe there is a *motionless center* which is the sustaining source of all the universal activities. Be this as it may, there is certainly in the heart of every man and woman a *selfless center* without which the outer man could not be, and the ignoring of which leads to suffering and confusion. This selfless center which takes the form, in the mind, of an *ideal of unselfishness* and spotless purity, the attainment of which is desirable, is man's eternal refuge from the storms of passion and all the conflicting elements of his lower nature. It is the Rock of Ages, the Christ within, the divine and immortal in all men.

As a man practices self-control he approximates more and more to this inward reality, and is less and less swayed by passion and grief, pleasure and pain, and lives a steadfast and virtuous life, manifesting manly strength and fortitude. The restraining of the passions, however, is merely the initial stage in self-discipline, and is immediately followed by the process of *Purification*. By this a man so purifies himself as to take passion out of the heart and mind altogether; not merely restraining it when it rises within him, but preventing it from rising altogether. By merely *restraining* his passions a man can never

arrive at peace, can never actualize his ideal; he must purify those passions.

It is in the purification of his lower nature that a man becomes strong and god-like, standing firmly upon the ideal center within, and rendering all temptations powerless and ineffectual. This purification is effected by thoughtful care, earnest meditation, and holy aspiration; and as success is achieved confusion of mind and life pass away, and calmness of mind and spiritualized conduct ensue.

True strength and power and usefulness are born of self-purification, for the lower animal forces are not lost, but are transmuted into intellectual and spiritual energy. The pure life (pure in thought and deed) is a life of conservation of energy; the impure life (even should the impurity not extend beyond thought) is a life of dissipation of energy. The pure man is more capable, and therefore more fit to succeed in his plans and to accomplish his purposes than the impure. Where the impure man fails, the pure man will step in and be victorious, because he directs his energies with a calmer mind and a greater definiteness and strength of purpose.

With the growth in purity, all the elements which constitute a strong and virtuous manhood are developed in an increasing degree of power, and as a man brings his lower nature into subjection, and makes his passions do his bidding, just so much will he mold the outer circumstances of his life, and influence others for good.

The third stage of self-discipline, that of *Relinquishment*, is a process of letting the lower desires and all impure and unworthy thoughts drop out of the mind, and also refusing to give them any admittance, leaving them to perish. As a man grows purer, he perceives that all evil is powerless, unless it receives his encouragement, and so he ignores it, and lets it pass out of his life. It is by pursuing this aspect of self-discipline that a man enters into and realizes the divine life, and manifests those qualities which are distinctly divine, such as wisdom, patience, non-resistance, compassion, and love. It is here, also, where a man becomes consciously immortal, rising above all the fluctuations and uncertainties of life, and living in an intelligent and unchangeable peace.

THE VIRTUE OF SELF-DISCIPLINE

By self-discipline a man attains to every degree of virtue and holiness, and finally becomes a purified son of God, realizing his oneness with the central heart of all things.

Without self-discipline a man drifts lower and lower, approximating more and more nearly to the beast, until at last he grovels, a lost creature, in the mire of his own befoulment. By self-discipline a man rises higher and higher, approximating more and more nearly to the divine, until at last he stands erect in his divine dignity, a saved soul, glorified by the radiance of his purity. Let a man discipline himself, and he will live; let a man cease to discipline himself, and he will perish. As a tree grows in beauty, health, and fruitfulness by being carefully pruned and tended, so a man grows in grace and beauty of life by cutting away all the branches of evil from his mind, and as he tends and develops the good by constant and unfailing effort.

As a man by practice acquires proficiency in his craft, so the earnest man acquires proficiency in goodness and wisdom. Men shrink from self-discipline because in its early stages it is painful and repellent, and the yielding to desire is, at first, sweet and inviting; but the end of desire is darkness and unrest, whereas the fruits of discipline are immortality and peace.

THE SECRET OF SUCCESS

Great men are they who see
that spiritual is stronger
than material force,
that thoughts rule the world.

—RALPH WALDO EMERSON

ALL THAT a man achieves and all that he fails to achieve is the direct result of his own thoughts. In a justly ordered universe, individual responsibility must be absolute. A man's weakness and strength, purity and impurity, are his own, and not another man's. They are brought about by himself, and not by another. They can only be altered by himself, never by another. His condition also is his own. His suffering and his happiness are evolved from within. As he thinks, so he is; as he continues to think, so he remains.

A strong man cannot help a weaker unless that weaker is willing to be helped, and even then the weak man must become strong of himself. He must, by his own efforts, develop the strength which he admires in another. None but himself can alter his condition.

It has been usual for men to think and to say, "Many men are slaves because one is an oppressor; let us hate the oppressor." Now, however, there is an increasing tendency to reverse this judgment, and to say, "One man is an oppressor because many are slaves; let us despise the slaves."

The truth is that oppressor and slave are co-operators in ignorance, and, while seeming to afflict each other, are in reality afflicting themselves. A perfect knowledge perceives the weakness of the oppressed and the misapplied power of the oppressor. A perfect love sees the suffering which each entails and condemns neither. A perfect compassion embraces oppressor and oppressed.

He who has conquered weakness, and has put away all self-ish thoughts, belongs neither to oppressor nor oppressed. He is free.

A man can only rise, conquer, and achieve by lifting up his thoughts. He can only remain weak, and abject, and miserable by refusing to lift up his thoughts.

THE IMPORTANCE OF PURPOSE

Until thought is linked with purpose there is no intelligent accomplishment. With the majority the ship of thought is allowed to "drift" upon the ocean of life. Aimlessness is a common vice, and such drifting must not continue for him who would steer clear of catastrophe and destruction.

They who have no central purpose in their life fall easy prey to petty worries, fears, troubles, and self-pityings, all of which are indications of weakness. All of which lead, just as surely as deliberately planned sins (though by a different route), to failure, unhappiness, and loss, for weakness cannot persist in a power-evolving universe.

A man should conceive of a legitimate purpose in his heart, and set out to accomplish it. He should make this purpose the centralizing point of his thoughts. It may take the form of a spiritual ideal, or it may be a worldly object, according to his nature at the time. But whichever it is, he should steadily focus his thought forces upon the object which he has set before him. He should make this purpose his supreme duty, and should devote himself to its attainment, not allowing his thoughts to wander away into short-lived fancies, longings, and imaginings. This is the royal road to self-control and true concentration of thought. Even if he fails again and again to accomplish his purpose (as he necessarily must until weakness is overcome),

the strength of character gained will be the measure of his true success, and this will form a new starting point in his life for future power and triumph.

Those who are not prepared for the apprehension of a great purpose, should fix their thoughts upon the faultless performance of their duty, no matter how insignificant their task may appear. Only in this way can their thoughts be gathered and focused, and resolution and energy be developed. Being focused and developed, there is nothing which they may not accomplish.

STRENGTHEN YOUR SPIRIT

Spiritual achievements are the consummation of holy aspirations. He who lives constantly in the conception of noble and lofty thoughts, who dwells upon all that is pure and unselfish, will, as surely as the sun reaches its zenith and the moon its full, become wise and noble in character, and rise into a position of influence and blessedness.

Achievement, of whatever kind, is the crown of effort, the diadem of thought. By the aid of self-control, resolution, purity, righteousness, and well-directed thought a man ascends. By the aid of animality, indolence, impurity, corruption, and confusion of thought a man descends.

A man who has risen to the heights of success in the world, and even to lofty altitudes in the spiritual realm, may descend into weakness and wretchedness by allowing arrogant, selfish, and corrupt thoughts to take possession of him.

Victories attained by right thought can only be maintained by watchfulness. Many give way when success is assured, and rapidly fall back into failure.

All achievements, whether in the business, intellectual, or

spiritual world, are the result of definitely directed thought, are governed by the same law, and are of the same method. The only difference lies in the object of attainment.

He who would accomplish little need sacrifice little, but he who would achieve much must sacrifice much.

WORK AND LIFE ARE THE SAME

Activity, both mental and physical, is the essence of life. The complete cessation of activity is death, and death is immediately followed by corruption. Ease and death are closely associated. The more there is of activity, the more abounding is life. The brain-worker, the original thinker, the man of unceasing mental activity, is the longest-lived man in the community; the agricultural laborer, the gardener, the man of unceasing physical activity, comes next with length of years.

. . .

There are those who are afraid of work, regarding it as an enemy, and who fear a breakdown by doing too much. They have to learn what a health-bestowing friend work is. Others are ashamed of work, looking upon it as a degrading thing to be avoided. The "pure in heart and sound in head" are neither afraid nor ashamed of work, and they dignify whatsoever they undertake. No necessary work can be degrading, but if a man regard his work as such, he is already degraded, not by his task, but by his slavish vanity.

. . .

The idle man who is afraid of work, and the vain man who is ashamed of it, are both on the way to poverty, if they are not already there. The industrious man, who loves work, and the man of true dignity, who glorifies work, are both on their way to affluence, if they are not already there. The lazy man

is sowing the seeds of poverty and crime; the vain man is sowing the seeds of humiliation and shame. The industrious man
is sowing the seeds of affluence and virtue; the dignified work-
er is sowing the seeds of victory and honor. Deeds are seeds,
and the harvest will appear in due season.

ELIMINATE THE NEGATIVE

The will to do springs from the knowledge that we can do.
Doubt and fear are the great enemies of knowledge, and he
who encourages them, who does not slay them, thwarts himself at every step.

He who has conquered doubt and fear has conquered failure. His every thought is allied with power, and all difficulties
are bravely met and wisely overcome. His purposes are season-
ably planted, and they bloom and bring forth fruit which does
not fall prematurely to the ground.

Thought allied fearlessly to purpose becomes creative force.
He who knows this is ready to become something higher and
stronger than a mere bundle of wavering thoughts and fluctu-
ating sensations. He who does this has become the conscious
and intelligent wielder of his mental powers.

THE MIND OF LOVE

If you love everything, you will perceive
the divine mystery in things.
Once you perceive it, you will begin
to comprehend it better every day.
And you will come at last to love
the whole world
with an all-embracing love.

FYODOR DOSTOYEVSKY

THE UNIVERSE is preserved because Love is at the Heart of it. Love is the only preservative power. Whilst there is hatred in the heart of man, he imagines the Law to be cruel, but when his heart is mellowed by Compassion and Love, he perceives that the Law is Infinite Kindness. So kind is the Law that it protects man against his own ignorance. Man, in his puny efforts to subvert the Law by attaching undue importance to his own little personality, brings upon himself such trains of suffering that he is at last compelled, in the depth of his afflictions, to seek for Wisdom; and finding Wisdom, he finds Love, and knows it as the Law of his being, the Law of the universe.

. . .

He who always acts from the spirit of Love is never deserted, is never left in a dilemma or difficulty, for Love (impersonal Love) is both Knowledge and Power. He who has learned how to Love has learned how to master every difficulty, how to transmute every failure into success, how to clothe every event and condition in garments of blessedness and beauty.

The way to Love is by self-mastery, and, travelling that way, a man builds himself up in Knowledge as he proceeds. Arriving at Love, he enters into full possession of body and mind, by right of the divine Power which he has earned.

"Perfect Love casteth out fear." To know Love is to know that there is no harmful power in the whole universe. Even sin itself, which the worldly and unbelieving imagine is so unconquerable, is known as a very weak and perishable thing, that shrinks away and disappears before the compelling power of Good. Perfect Love is perfect Harmlessness. And he who has destroyed, in himself, all thoughts of harm, and all desire to harm, receives the universal protection, and knows himself to be invincible.

TO LIVE IN LOVE

To live in Love is to work in Joy. Love is the magic that transforms all things into power and beauty. It brings plenty out of poverty, power out of weakness, loveliness out of deformity, sweetness out of bitterness, light out of darkness, and produces all blissful conditions out of its own substantial but indefinable essence.

He who loves can never want. The universe belongs to Goodness, and it therefore belongs to the good man. It can be possessed by all without stint or shrinking, for Goodness, and the abundance of Goodness (material, mental, and spiritual abundance), is inexhaustible. Think lovingly, speak lovingly, act lovingly, and your every need shall be supplied; you shall not walk in desert places, and no danger shall overtake you.

Love sees with faultless vision, judges true judgment, acts in wisdom. Look through the eyes of Love, and you shall see everywhere the Beautiful and True; judge with the mind of Love, and you shall err not, shall wake no wail of sorrow; act in the spirit of Love, and you shall strike undying harmonies upon the Harp of Life.

Make no compromise with self. Cease not to strive until your whole being is swallowed up in Love. To love all and always—this is the Heaven of heavens.

Perfect Love is perfect Patience. Anger and irritability cannot dwell with it nor come near it. It sweetens every bitter occasion with the perfume of holiness, and transmutes trial into divine strength. Complaint is foreign to it. He who loves bewails nothing, but accepts all things and conditions as heavenly guests; he is therefore constantly blessed, and sorrow does not overtake him.

Perfect Love is perfect Trust. He who has destroyed the desire to grasp can never be troubled with the fear of loss. Loss and gain are alike foreign to him. Steadfastly maintaining a loving attitude of mind toward all, and pursuing, in the performance of his duties, a constant and loving activity, Love protects him and evermore supplies him in fullest measure with all that he needs.

Perfect Love is perfect Power. The wisely loving heart commands without exercising any authority. All things and all men obey him who obeys the Highest. He thinks, and lo! he has already accomplished! He speaks, and behold! a world hangs upon his simple utterances! He has harmonized his thoughts with the Imperishable and Unconquerable Forces, and for him weakness and uncertainty are no more. His every thought is a purpose; his every act an accomplishment; he moves with the Great Law, not setting his puny personal will against it, and he thus becomes a channel through which the Divine Power can flow in unimpeded and beneficent expression. He has thus become Power itself.

Perfect Love is perfect Wisdom. The man who loves all is the man who knows all. Having thoroughly learned the lessons of his own heart, he knows the tasks and trials of other hearts, and adapts himself to them gently and without ostentation.

Love illuminates the intellect; without it the intellect is blind and cold and lifeless. Love succeeds where the intellect fails; sees where the intellect is blind; knows where the intellect is ignorant. Reason is only completed in Love, and is ultimately absorbed in it. Love is the Supreme Reality in the universe, and as such it contains all Truth. Infinite Tenderness enfolds and cherishes the universe; therefore is the wise man gentle and childlike and tender-hearted. He sees that the one thing which all creatures need is Love, and he gives unstintingly. He knows that all occasions require the adjusting power of Love, and he ceases from harshness.

To the eye of Love all things are revealed, not as an infinity of complex effects, but in the light of Eternal Principles, out of which spring all causes and effects, and back into which they return. "God is Love"; therefore than Love there is nothing more perfect. He who would find pure Knowledge let him find pure Love.

Perfect Love is perfect Peace. He who dwells with it has completed his pilgrimage in the underworld of sorrow. With mind calm and heart at rest, he has banished the shadows of grief, and knows the deathless Life.

SELFLESS LOVE: THE HIDDEN TRUTH

It is said that Michelangelo saw in every rough block of stone a thing of beauty awaiting the master-hand to bring it into reality. Even so, within each there reposes the Divine Image awaiting the master-hand of Faith and the chisel of Patience to bring it into manifestation. And that Divine Image is revealed and realized as stainless, selfless Love.

Hidden deep in every human heart is the spirit of Divine Love, whose holy and spotless essence is undying and eternal.

It is the Truth in man; it is that which belongs to the Supreme: that which is real and immortal. All else changes and passes away; this alone is permanent and imperishable; and to realize this Love by ceaseless diligence in the practice of the highest righteousness, to live in it and to become fully conscious in it, is to enter into immortality here and now, is to become one with Truth, one with God, one with the central Heart of all things, and to know our own divine and eternal nature.

He who strives to reach and to accomplish the Divine will be tried to the very uttermost. But he who has resolutely set himself to realize the Highest recognizes no such thing as defeat. Every slip, every fall, every return to selfishness is a lesson learned, an experience gained, from which a golden grain of wisdom is extracted, helping the striver toward the accomplishment of his lofty object. To recognize

> "That of our vices we can frame
> A ladder if we will but tread
> Beneath our feet each deed of shame,"

is to enter the way that leads unmistakably towards the Divine, and the failings of one who thus recognizes are so many dead selves, upon which he rises . . . to higher things.

THE WAY OF WISDOM

The price of wisdom is above pearls.

JOB 28:18 (RSVB)

THE PATH OF WISDOM is the highest way, the way in which all doubt and uncertainty are dispelled and knowledge and surety are realized.

Amid the excitements and pleasures of the world and the surging whirlpools of human passions, Wisdom—so calm, so silent and so beautiful—is indeed difficult to find, difficult, not because of its incomprehensible complexity, but because of its unobtrusive simplicity, and because self is so blind and rash, and so jealous of its rights and pleasures.

Wisdom is "rejected of men" because it always comes right home to one's self in the form of wounding reproof, and the lower nature of man cannot bear to be reproved. Before Wisdom can be acquired, self must be wounded to the death, and because of this, because Wisdom is the enemy of self, self rises in rebellion, and will not be overcome and denied.

The foolish man is governed by his passions and personal cravings, and when about to do anything he does not ask "Is this right?" but only considers how much pleasure or personal advantage he will gain by it. He does not govern his passions and act from fixed principles, but is the slave of his inclinations and follows where they lead.

The wise man governs his passions and puts away all personal cravings. He never acts from impulse and passion, but dispassionately considers what is right to be done, and does it. He is always thoughtful and self-possessed, and guides his conduct by the loftiest moral principles. He is superior to both pleasure and pain.

Wisdom cannot be found in books or travel, in learning or philosophy, it is *acquired by practice only*. A man may read the precepts of the greatest sages continually, but if he does not purify and govern himself he will remain foolish. A man may be intimately conversant with the writings of the greatest philosophers, but so long as he continues to give way to his passions he will not attain to wisdom.

Wisdom is right action, right doing; folly is wrong action, wrong doing. All reading, all study, all learning is vain if a man will not see his errors and give them up. Wisdom says to the vain man, "Do not praise yourself," to the proud man, "Humble yourself," to the gossip, "Govern your tongue," to the angry man, "Subdue your anger," to the resentful man, "Forgive your enemy," to the self-indulgent man, "Be temperate," to the impure man, "Purge your heart of lust," and to all men, "Beware of small faults, do your own duty faithfully, and never intermeddle with the duty of another."

These things are very simple; the doing of them is simple, but as it leads to the annihilation of self, the selfish tendencies in man object to them and rise up in revolt against them, loving their own life of turbulent excitement and feverish pleasure, and hating the calm and beautiful silence of Wisdom. Thus men remain in folly.

Nevertheless, the Way of Wisdom is always open, is always ready to receive the tread of the pilgrim who has grown weary of the thorny and intricate ways of folly. No man is prevented from becoming wise but by himself; no man can acquire Wisdom but by his own exertions; and he who is prepared to be honest with himself, to measure the depths of his ignorance, to come face to face with his errors, to recognize and acknowledge his faults, and at once to set about the task of his own regeneration, such a man will find the way of Wisdom, walking which with humble and obedient feet, he will in due time come to the sweet City of Deliverance.

THE UNFAILING WISDOM

A man should be superior to his possessions, his body, his circumstances and surroundings, and the opinions of others and their attitude towards him. Until he is this, he is not strong and steadfast. He should also rise superior to his own desires and opinions; and until he is this, he is not wise.

The man who identifies himself with his possessions will feel that all is lost when these are lost; he who regards himself as the outcome and the tool of circumstances will weakly fluctuate with every change in his outward condition; and great will be his unrest and pain who seeks to stand upon the approbation of others.

To detach oneself from every outward thing and to rest securely upon the inward Virtue—this is the Unfailing Wisdom. Having this Wisdom, a man will be the same whether in riches or poverty. The one cannot add to his strength, nor the other rob him of his serenity. Neither can riches defile him who has washed away all the inward defilement, nor the lack of them degrade him who has ceased to degrade the temple of his soul.

To refuse to be enslaved by any outward thing or happening, regarding all such things and happenings as for your use, for your education, this is Wisdom. To the wise all occurrences are *good*, and, having no eye for evil, they grow wiser every day. They utilize all things, and thus put all things under their feet. They see all their mistakes as soon as made, and accept them as lessons of intrinsic value, knowing that there are no mistakes in the Divine Order. They thus rapidly approach the Divine Perfection. They are moved by none, yet learn from all. They crave love from none, yet give love to all. To learn, and not to be shaken; to love where one is not loved; herein lies the strength which shall never fail a man. The man who says in his heart, "I will teach all men, and learn from none," will neither teach nor learn whilst he is in that frame of mind, but will remain in his folly.

All strength and wisdom and power and knowledge a man will find within himself, but he will not find it in egotism; he will only find it in obedience, submission, and willingness to learn. He must obey the Higher, and not glorify himself in the lower. He who stands upon egotism, rejecting reproof, instruction, and the lessons of experience, will surely fall; yea, he is already fallen. Said a great Teacher to his disciples, "Those who shall be a lamp unto themselves, relying upon themselves only, and not relying upon any external help, but holding fast to the Truth as their lamp, and, seeking their salvation in the Truth alone, shall not look for assistance to any besides themselves, it is they among my disciples who shall reach the very topmost height! *But they must be willing to learn.*" The wise man is always anxious to learn, but never anxious to teach, for he knows that the true Teacher is in the heart of every man, and must ultimately be found there by all. The foolish man, being governed largely by vanity, is very anxious to teach, but unwilling to learn, not having found the Holy Teacher within who speaks wisdom to the humbly listening soul. Be self-reliant, but let thy self-reliance be saintly and not selfish.

Folly and wisdom, weakness and strength are within a man,

and not in any external thing, neither do they spring from any external cause. A man cannot be strong for another, he can only be strong for himself; he cannot overcome for another, he can only overcome of himself. You may learn of another, but you must accomplish for yourself. Put away all external props, and rely upon the Truth within you. A creed will not bear a man up in the hour of temptation; he must possess the inward Knowledge which slays temptation. A speculative philosophy will prove a shadowy thing in the time of calamity; a man must have the inward Wisdom which puts an end to grief.

Goodness, which is the aim of all religions, is distinct from religions themselves. Wisdom, which is the aim of every philosophy, is distinct from all philosophies. The Unfailing Wisdom is found only by constant practice in pure thinking and well-doing; by harmonizing one's mind and heart to those things which are beautiful, lovable, and true.

WISDOM IS FREEDOM

Wisdom is many-sided. The wise man adapts himself to others. He acts for their good, yet never violates the moral virtues or the principles of right conduct. The foolish man cannot adapt himself to others; he acts for himself only, and continually violates the moral virtues and the principles of right conduct. There is a degree of wisdom in every act of impartiality, and once a man has touched and experienced the impartial zone, he can recover it again and again, until he finally establishes himself in it.

Every thought, word, or act of wisdom tells on the world at large, for it is fraught with greatness. Wisdom is a well of knowledge and a spring of power. It is profound and comprehensive, and is so exact and all-inclusive as to embrace the smallest details. In its spacious greatness it does not overlook the small. The wise mind is like the world: it contains all things in their proper place and order, and is not burdened thereby. Like the world, also, it is free, and unconscious of any restrictions; yet it is never loose, never erring, never sinful and repentant. Wisdom is the steady, grown-up being of whom folly was the crying infant. It has outgrown the weakness and dependence, the errors and punishments of infantile ignorance, and is erect, poised, strong, and serene.

The understanding mind needs no external support. It stands of itself on the firm ground of knowledge; not book knowledge, but ripened experience. It has passed through all minds, and therefore knows them. It has travelled with all hearts, and knows their journeyings in joy and sorrow.

When wisdom touches a man, he is lifted up and transfigured. He becomes a new being, with new aims and powers, and he inhabits a new universe in which to accomplish a new and glorious destiny.

VISIONS OF BEAUTY

Those who dream by day
are cognizant of many things
which escape those
who dream only by night.

EDGAR ALLAN POE

THE DREAMERS are the saviors of the world. As the visible world is sustained by the invisible, so men, through all their trials and sins and sordid vocations, are nourished by the beautiful visions of their individual dreamers.

Humanity cannot forget its dreamers; it cannot let their ideals fade and die; it lives in them; it knows them as the realities which it shall one day see and know.

Composer, sculptor, painter, poet, prophet, and sage, these are the makers of the afterworld, the architects of heaven. The world is beautiful because they have lived; without them, laboring humanity would perish.

He who cherishes a beautiful vision, a lofty ideal in his heart, will one day realize it.

Columbus cherished a vision of another world, and he discovered it.

Copernicus fostered the vision of a multiplicity of worlds, and he revealed it.

Gautama Buddha beheld the vision of a spiritual world of stainless beauty and perfect peace, and he entered into it.

Cherish your visions; cherish your ideals; cherish the music that stirs in your heart, the beauty that forms in your mind, the loveliness that drapes your purest thoughts. Out of them will grow all delightful conditions, all heavenly environment. Of them, if you but remain true to them, your world will at last be built.

To desire is to obtain; to aspire is to achieve. Shall man's basest desires receive the fullest measure of gratification, and his purest aspirations starve for lack of sustenance? Such is not the law. Such a condition of things can never be.

Dream lofty dreams, and as you dream, so shall you become. Your vision is the promise of what you shall one day be; your ideal is the prophecy of what you shall at last unveil.

THE POWER OF AN IDEA

You will become as small as your controlling desire; as great as your dominant aspiration. In the words of Stanton Kirkham Davis, "You may be keeping accounts, and presently you shall walk out the door that for so long has seemed to you the barrier of your ideals, and shall find yourself before an audience— the pen still behind your ear, the ink stains on your fingers— and then and there shall pour out the torrent of your inspiration. You may be driving sheep, and you shall wander to the city—innocent and openmouthed; you shall wander under the bold guidance of the spirit into the studio of the master, and after a time he shall say, 'I have nothing more to teach you.' And now you have become the master, who did so recently dream of great things while driving sheep. You shall lay down your staff to take upon yourself the regeneration of the world."

LOOK INWARD FOR INSPIRATION

The greatest achievements were at first and for a time dreams. The oak sleeps in the acorn; the bird waits in the egg, and a waking angel stirs in the highest vision of the soul. Dreams are the seedlings of realities.

Your circumstances may be uncongenial, but they shall not long remain so if you but perceive an ideal and strive to reach it. You cannot travel within and stand still without.

Here is a youth hard pressed by poverty and labor; confined long hours in an unhealthy workshop; unschooled, and lacking all the arts of refinement. But he dreams of better things. He thinks of intelligence, of refinement, of grace and beauty. He conceives of and mentally builds up an ideal condition of life. The vision of a wider liberty and a larger scope takes possession of him. Unrest urges him to action, and he utilizes all his spare time and means to the development of his latent powers and resources.

Very soon so altered has his mind become that the workshop can no longer hold him. It has become so out of harmony with his mentality that it falls out of his life as a garment is cast aside, and, with the growth of opportunities which fit the scope of his expanding powers, he passes out of it forever.

A MASTER OF FORCES

Years later we see this youth as a full-grown man. We find him a master of certain forces of the mind which he wields with world-wide influence and almost unequaled power. In his hands he holds the cords of gigantic responsibilities. He speaks, and lives are changed; men and women hang upon his words and thoughts and remold their characters; sunlike, he becomes the fixed and luminous center around which innumerable destinies revolve.

He has realized the vision of his youth. He has become one with his ideal. And you, too, will realize the vision (not the idle wish) of your heart, be it base or beautiful, or a mixture of the two, for you will always gravitate toward that which you most love. In your hands will be placed the exact results of your own thoughts; you will receive what you earn; no more, no less. Whatever your present environment may be, you will fall, remain, or rise with your thoughts, your vision, your ideal.

THERE IS NO SUCH THING AS "LUCK"

The thoughtless, the ignorant, and the indolent, seeing only the apparent effects of things and not the things themselves, talk of luck, of fortune, and chance. Seeing a man grow rich, they say, "How lucky he is!" Observing another become intellectual, they exclaim, "How highly favored he is!" And noting the saintly character and wide influence of another, they remark, "How chance aids him at every turn!"

They do not see the trials and failures and struggles which these men have voluntarily encountered in order to gain their experience. They have no knowledge of the sacrifices these men have made, of the undaunted efforts they have put forth, of the faith they have exercised, that they might overcome the apparently insurmountable, and realize the vision of their hearts.

They do not know the darkness and the heartaches; they only see the light and joy, and call it "luck." They do not see the long and arduous journey, but only behold the pleasant goal, and call it "good fortune." They do not understand the process, but only perceive the result, and call it "chance."

In all human affairs there are efforts, and there are results, and the strength of the effort is the measure of the result. Chance is not. Gifts; powers; material, intellectual, and spiritual possessions, are the fruits of effort; they are thoughts completed, objects accomplished, visions realized.

The vision that you glorify in your mind, the ideal that you enthrone in your heart—this you will build your life by, this you will become.

YOUR ASPIRATIONS SHAPE YOUR LIFE

What you are, so is your world. Everything in the universe is resolved into your own inward experience. It matters little what is without, for it is all a reflection of your own state of consciousness. It matters everything what you are within, for everything without will be mirrored and colored accordingly.

All that you positively know is contained in your own experience; all that you ever will know must pass through the gateway of experience, and so become part of yourself.

Your own thoughts, desires, and aspirations comprise your world, and, to you, all that there is in the universe of beauty and joy and bliss, or of ugliness and sorrow and pain, is contained within yourself. By your own thoughts you make or mar your life, your world, your universe. As you build within by the power of thought, so will your outward life and circumstances shape themselves accordingly. Whatsoever you harbor in the inmost chambers of your heart will, sooner or later by the inevitable law of reaction, shape itself in your outward life. The soul that is impure, sordid and selfish, is gravitating with unerring precision toward misfortune and catastrophe; the soul that is pure, unselfish, and noble, is gravitating with equal precision toward happiness and prosperity. Every soul attracts its own, and nothing can possibly come to it that does not belong to it. To realize this is to recognize the universality of Divine Law. The incidents of every human life, which both make and mar, are drawn to it by the quality and power of its own inner thought-life. Every soul is a complex combination of gathered experiences and thoughts, and the body is but an improvised vehicle for its manifestation. What, therefore, your thoughts are, that is your real self; and the world around, both animate and inanimate, wears the aspect with which your thoughts clothe it. "All that we are is the result of what we have thought; it is founded on our thoughts; it is made up of our thoughts." Thus said Buddha, and it therefore follows that if a man is happy, it is because he dwells in happy thoughts; if miserable, because he dwells in despondent and debilitating thoughts. Whether one be fearful or fearless, foolish or wise, troubled or serene, within that soul lies the cause of its own state or states, and never without.

PEACE OF MIND

Heaven is to be at peace with things. . . .

GEORGE SANTAYANA

CALMNESS OF MIND is one of the beautiful jewels of wisdom. It is the result of long and patient effort in self-control. Its presence is an indication of ripened experience, and of a more than ordinary knowledge of the laws and operations of thought.

A man becomes calm in the measure that he understands himself as a thought-evolved being. This knowledge necessitates the understanding of others as the result of thought. And as he develops a right understanding, and sees more and more clearly the internal relations of things by the action of cause and effect, he ceases to fuss and fume and worry and grieve, and remains poised, steadfast, and serene.

The happy man, having learned how to govern himself, knows how to adapt himself to others; and they, in turn, revere his spiritual strength, and feel that they can learn of him and rely upon him. The more tranquil a man becomes, the greater is his success, his influence, his power for good. Even the ordinary businessman finds his business prosperity increases as he develops a greater self-control and equanimity. For people always prefer to deal with a man whose behavior is equable.

The strong, calm man is always loved and revered. He is like a shade-giving tree in a thirsty land, or a sheltering rock in a storm. Who does not love a tranquil heart, a sweet-tempered, balanced disposition? It does not matter whether it rains or shines, or what changes come to those possessing these blessings, for they are always sweet, serene, and calm.

That exquisite poise of character which we call serenity is the final lesson of culture; it is the flowering of life, the fruit of the soul. It is as precious as wisdom, more to be desired than gold—yes, even than fine gold.

How insignificant money-seeking looks in comparison with a happy life—a life that dwells in the ocean of truth, beneath the waves, beyond the reach of tempests, in the eternal calm!

TAKE COMMAND OF YOURSELF

He only finds peace who conquers himself, who strives, day by day, after greater self-possession, greater self-control, greater calmness of mind. One can only be a joy to himself and a blessing to others in the measure that he has command of himself; and such self-command is gained only by persistent practice. A man must conquer his weaknesses by daily effort; he must understand them and study how to eliminate them from his character; and if he continues to strive, not giving way, he will gradually become victorious; and each little victory gained (though there is a sense in which no victory can be called *little*) will be so much more calmness acquired and added to his character as an eternal possession. He will thus make himself strong and capable and blessed, fit to perform his duties faultlessly, and to meet all events with an untroubled spirit. But even if he does not, in this life, reach that supreme calm which no shock can disturb, he will become sufficiently self-possessed and pure to enable him to fight the battle of life fearlessly, and to leave the world a little richer for having known the benignity of his presence.

How many people we know who sour their lives, who destroy their poise of character, who ruin all that is sweet and beautiful by explosive tempers! It is a question of whether or not the great majority of people do not ruin their lives and mar their happiness by lack of self-control. How few people we meet in life who are well-balanced, who have that exquisite poise which is characteristic of the finished character!

Yes, humanity surges with uncontrolled passion, is tumultuous with ungoverned grief, is blown about by anxiety and doubt. Only the wise man, only he whose thoughts are controlled and purified, makes the winds and storms of the soul obey him.

Tempest-tossed souls, wherever you may be, under whatsoever conditions you may live, know this—in the ocean of life the isles of blessedness are smiling, and the sunny shore of your ideal awaits your coming. Keep your hand firmly upon the helm of thought. In the ship of your soul reclines the commanding master. He does but sleep; wake him.

THE PATH TO PEACE

Amid the multitude of conflicting opinions and theories, and caught in the struggle of existence, whither shall the confused truthseeker turn to find the path that leads to peace unending? To what refuge shall he fly from the uncertainties and sorrows of change?

Will he find peace in pleasure? Pleasure has its place, and in its place it is good; but as an end, as a refuge, it affords no shelter, and he who seeks it as such does but increase the anguish of life; for what is more fleeting than pleasure, and what is more empty than the heart that seeks satisfaction in so ephemeral a thing? There is, therefore, no abiding refuge in pleasure.

Will he find peace in wealth and worldly success? Wealth and worldly success have their place, but they are fickle and uncertain possessions, and he who seeks them for themselves alone will be burdened with many anxieties and cares. . . . There is no abiding refuge in wealth and worldly success.

Will he find peace in health? Health has its place, and it should not be thrown away or despised, but it belongs to the body which is destined for dissolution, and is therefore perishable. Even should health be maintained for a hundred years, the time will come when the physical energies will decline and debility and decay will overtake them. There is no abiding refuge in health.

Will he find refuge in those whom he dearly loves? Those whom he loves have their place in his life. They afford him means of practicing unselfishness, and therefore of arriving at Truth. He should cherish them with loving care, and consider their needs before his own; but the time will come when they will be separated from him, and he will be left alone. There is no abiding refuge in loved ones.

Will he find peace in this Scripture or that? Scripture fills an important place. As a guide it is good, but it cannot be a refuge, for one may know the Scripture by heart, and yet be in sore conflict and unrest. The theories of men are subject to successive changes, and no limit can be set to the variety of textual interpretations. There is no abiding refuge in Scripture.

Will he find peace in solitude? Solitude is good and necessary in its place, but he who courts it as a lasting refuge will be like one perishing of thirst in a waterless desert. He will escape men and the turmoil of the city, but he will not escape himself and the unrest of his heart. There is no abiding rest in solitude.

If, then, the seeker can find no refuge in pleasure, in success, in health, in friends, in Scripture, in the teacher, or in solitude, whither shall he turn to find that sanctuary which shall afford abiding peace?

Let him take refuge in righteousness; let him fly to the sanctuary of a purified heart. Let him enter the pathway of a blameless, stainless life, and walk it meekly and patiently until it brings him to the eternal temple of Truth in his own heart.

He who has taken refuge in Truth, even in the habitation of a wise understanding and a loving and steadfast heart, is the same whether in pleasure or pain; wealth or poverty; success or failure; health or sickness; with friends or without; in solitude or noisy haunts; and he is independent of bibles and teachers, for the Spirit of Truth instructs him. He perceives, without fear or sorrow, the change and decay which are in all things. He has found peace; he has entered the abiding sanctuary; he knows the Light that will never go out.

WAR AND PEACE

To fight against war is to produce war. It is impossible to fight for peace, because all fighting is the annihilation of peace. To think of putting an end to war by denouncing and fighting it is the same as if one should try to quench fire by throwing straw upon it. He, therefore, who is truly a man of peace, does not resist war, but practices peace. He who takes sides and practices attack and defense, is responsible for war, for he is always at war in his mind. He cannot know the nature of peace, for he has not arrived at peace in his own heart. The true man of peace is he who has put away from his mind the spirit of quarreling and party strife, who neither attacks others nor defends himself, and whose heart is at peace with all. Such a man has already laid in his heart the foundations of the empire of peace; he is a peace maker, for he is at peace with the whole world and practices the spirit of peace under all circumstances.

Very beautiful is the spirit of peace, and it says, "Come and rest." Bickerings, quarrellings, party divisions—these must be forever abandoned by him who would establish peace.

War will continue so long as men will allow themselves, individually, to be dominated by passion, and only when men have quelled the inward tumult will the outward horror pass away.

Self is the great enemy, the producer of all strife, and the maker of many sorrows; he, therefore, who will bring about peace on earth, let him overcome egotism, let him subdue his passions, let him conquer himself.

THE GLORIOUS CONQUEST

Truth can only be apprehended by the conquest of self.

Blessedness can only be arrived at by overcoming the lower nature.

The way of Truth is barred by a man's self.

The only enemies that can actually hinder him are his own passions and delusions.

Until a man realizes this, and commences to cleanse his heart, he has not found the Path which leads to knowledge and peace.

Set at Westcott & Thomson Inc. in Monotype Perpetua,
a classic type-face designed in 1922
by Eric Gill, sculptor and engraver.
Printed on Hallmark Eggshell Book paper,
Designed by Bruce Baker.